D0576930

Freight Trains

by Peter Brady

Bridgestone Books

an Imprint of Capstone Press

Bridgestone Books are published by Capstone Press
818 North Willow Street, Mankato, Minnesota 56001
Copyright © 1996 by Capstone Press
Printed in the United States of America

Library of Congress Cataloging-in-Publication Data
Brady, Peter. 1944–
    Freight trains/Peter Brady
    p. cm.
    Includes bibliographical references and index.
    Summary: Describes various kinds of train cars including the boxcar, livestock car, and
flatcar.
    ISBN 1-56065-349-3
    1. Railroads--Juvenile literature. [1. Railroads.] I. Title.
TF148.B696 1996
625.1--dc20

                        95-47766
                           CIP
                            AC

Photo credits
All photos by Stokka Productions of Mankato, Minnesota

Table of Contents

Words in **boldface** type in the text are defined in the Words to Know section in the back of this book.

Freight Trains

Freight trains carry things from place to place. The things they carry are called **goods**. Freight trains never carry **passengers**.

The Locomotive

The engineer sits in the locomotive. It pulls the train. Freight train locomotives have **diesel engines**.

The Boxcar

The boxcar carries goods that fit in boxes or crates. It shelters goods from the weather. Boxcars are loaded and unloaded through sliding doors.

SOO LINE
29667
CAPY   80000
LD LMT   00
LT WT   00

The Livestock Car

The livestock car carries animals. It has openings along the sides so the animals can breathe fresh air. Cows and pigs go to **market** in livestock cars.

The Gondola Car

The gondola car has an open top and low sides. It carries heavy goods. Steel beams, concrete pipes, and scrap metal are carried on gondola cars.

The Hopper Car

The hopper car carries coal, grain, sand, and other loose goods. Goods are loaded through the top of the hopper car and unloaded from the bottom.

The Tank Car

The tank car carries liquids and gases. Oil is carried in tank cars. Chemicals are carried in tank cars, too.

The Flatcar

The flatcar has no top and no sides. It carries large goods that do not fit in other cars. Bulldozers and semitrailers ride on flatcars.

The Caboose

The caboose is the very last car in the train. It is where the **crew** stays. A freight train with a small crew does not have a caboose.

Hands On: Make a Train Whistle

Trains send signals with their whistles. The different signals mean different things.

- One long whistle means the train is coming into the station.
- One short whistle means stop.
- Two short whistles mean the train is going to move.
- Three short whistles mean the train is backing up.
- Many short whistles in a row mean get off the tracks.

To make your own train whistle, you will need one empty plastic soda pop bottle. Make sure it is clean and dry.

Make your whistle toot like a real train whistle by blowing across the top of the bottle.

Words to Know

crew—people who work on a train

diesel engine—an engine that runs on diesel fuel rather than gasoline

goods—all the things people use, from food to computers to toys

market—a place where people gather to buy and sell goods, including animals

passengers—people who ride a train but do not help operate it

Read More

Ammon, Richard. *Trains at Work.* New York: Atheneum, 1993.

Gibbons, Gail. *Trains.* New York: Holiday House, 1987.

Pierce, Jack. *The Freight Train Book.* Minneapolis: Carolrhoda Books, 1980.

Rockwell, Anne. *Trains.* New York: E.P. Dutton, 1988.

Index